S. Goodall

Confident
Classroom
Leadership

Confident
Classroom
Leadership

PETER HOOK AND ANDY VASS

David Fulton Publishers
London

David Fulton Publishers Ltd
Ormond House, 26–27 Boswell Street, London WC1N 3JD
http://www.fultonbooks.co.uk

First published in Great Britain by David Fulton Publishers 2000
Reprinted 2000

British Library Cataloguing in Publication Data
A catalogue record for this book is available from the British Library

ISBN 1-85346-686-7

Typeset by FSH Ltd, London
Printed in Great Britain by Bell and Bain Ltd, Glasgow

CONTENTS

Acknowledgements   vii

Some thoughts   ix

How to use this book   xi

Introduction Beginning the journey   1

Chapter 1   Becoming a leader in your classroom   5

Chapter 2   The emotional climate   17

Chapter 3   Establishing your classroom agenda   29

Chapter 4   The power of language   45

Chapter 5   Essential protocols   61

Chapter 6   Putting it into practice   67

References and resources   81

ACKNOWLEDGEMENTS

We would like to thank

- all the thousands of teachers and students we have worked with in our schools and on our workshops. Their opinions and feedback have created this book;

- Bill Rogers, an inspirational teacher and a good friend. We are indebted to Bill for his unique gift of showing us how to express what we have always done and always believed in. *'Good on yer, mate'*;

- CEM and, in particular, Rod Smith for their professionalism, commitment and support;

- David Fulton for being quite unfazed by getting a book published in record time and for the confidence that we could do it;

- Paula Barron for the loan of her tranquil and beautiful house to hide in while we wrote the book.

We are both omnivorous learners and our journey to this book has been eclectic to say the least. We have had the privilege of learning with some of the best teachers we have ever seen. We have tried to acknowledge their influences and if we have omitted any, it is not deliberate on our part. If you recognise an idea here that we haven't credited you with, please let us know and we will make amends in the next book.

Peter would like to thank

- My wife Janet (the first true and inspirational classroom leader that I met) and children Neil, Alan, Ian and Brian for support and patience;

- Peter Wilkinson for tolerating me while I learnt my craft;

- all of the students and teachers that I have worked with, but especially Janice and the students of Class 6 for allowing me to take part in their very special magic.

Andy would like to thank

- my wife Sue and children Jenny, Jack and Andy for unstinting faith and coping with not seeing Dad for far too long;

- Rob Probin and Phil Harding for always being there, for convincing me that I could do it and for making risks turn into fun;

- the individual students that I have worked with, for their grace and patience in running with new ideas and for their responses which taught me that what I believe and what is contained here is true;

- some amazing teachers of Neuro Linguistic Programming (NLP) – Richard Bandler, Don Blackerby, Michael Breen and Ian McDermott.

SOME THOUGHTS...

Let people realise clearly that every time they threaten someone, humiliate, hurt unnecessarily, dominate or reject another human being, they become forces for the creation of a psychopathology even if these be small forces. Let them recognise that everyone who is kind, helpful, decent, psychologically democratic, affectionate and warm is a therapeutic force though a small one.

Abraham Maslow

Hope is a waking dream.

Aristotle

Whatever you can do or dream you can, begin it. Boldness has genius, power and magic in it. Begin it now!

Goethe

You've got to help me. You've got to hold out your hand even when that's the last thing I seem to want or need. Each time you are kind and gentle and encouraging, each time you try to understand because you really care, my heart begins to grow wings, very small wings, very feeble wings – but wings.

Don Peretz Elkins

HOW TO USE THIS BOOK

- Make the information here relevant to you. There is a wide margin for writing ideas, jotting key words down or noting some personal responses to questions posed both within the text and in the activity sheets.

- At the end of the chapter there are 'Questions for professional development'. These may be used as part of your portfolio.

Start by getting the big picture

- Scan through the book, stopping wherever you get the urge to do so. Look at the contents page and the key point summaries towards the end of each chapter. Do whatever it takes for you to get a feel for what the book can do for you.

- Begin to make connections between the ideas, strategies and skills contained in the book and aspects of your own experience. How will what is on offer here support you in your classroom? In what ways does it match or connect with what you know already? What ideas are unusual or different to how you behave in class?

Formulate your own goals

- What is it *specifically* you want to know from this book? What would you need to know to become even better at what you do?

- What kind of things would you like to be able to do as a classroom leader?

Give us feedback

We are genuinely keen to receive

- *any* feedback and will make every effort to include it in newsletters, subsequent editions or other books;

- further questions you may have;

- experiences of implementing the strategies;

- any successful ideas or variations you have discovered;

- ideas that haven't worked (yet!)

Please contact us by E-mail:
PeterHook@phtc.demon.co.uk

or

andy@munrotraining.freeserve.co.uk

or by post:
Andy Vass or Peter Hook
c/o CEM, Red Lion House,
9–10 High Street,
High Wycombe,
Bucks., HP11 2AZ

Introduction

BEGINNING THE JOURNEY

If you are doing something that doesn't work, the more you do it or the harder you try to do it the more it doesn't work.

Richard Bandler

Welcome to the first part of what we hope will be an even more stimulating, enjoyable and rewarding future in teaching. An opportunity to make a real difference to your students. What greater challenge can anyone have than to make a positive difference, however small, to someone's life and what greater satisfaction comes from that knowledge?

You may think now of people who created that small (or major) therapeutic force in your life. Who were your favourite teachers, the ones who inspired you and made you feel important? The ones who you saw as having confidence in you, who made the time to listen and valued what you said. As you think of those people, what was it about them that can still create these emotions in you? Of course they had a style and manner of working with their students and obviously the things they said and the way they said them made a big difference.

What we're asking you to consider now is...

- **What beliefs did they hold that allowed them to be this way?**

- **What were the values that directed their behaviour?**

- **How were they able to create for themselves the physical state and intellectual frame of mind to persistently and unconditionally create that spark in you and many others?**

- **What part of them did they allow you access to?**

Our belief is that these people you have been thinking about had one thing in common. They believed with a passion that what they were doing was right. They had a vision of how they wanted the emotional, intellectual and physical climate of their classrooms to be. They articulated and lived those beliefs and visions – they 'walked the talk'. They also had realistic beliefs about what teachers do. They appreciated the personal qualities they possessed. They understood how these supported and encouraged them in their classroom leadership. Most of all, they passionately cared about how to help their students become 'winners'.

There is enough information in this book, not only in terms of practical strategies and skills, but also underpinned by user-friendly theory and explanations, to effectively sustain and support you through your development of the skills of classroom leadership. However, learning is not a finite process and as your career progresses, additional skills and understandings are required. For this reason *Confident Classroom Leadership* is the first of a trilogy of books supporting your professional development. Moving coherently on from where you are now, *Winning Classrooms* and *Teaching with Influence* will provide key skills and insights to maintain your progress as your role continues to develop.

It may seem obvious, but it's important to remember that teaching is a naturally stressful profession. Can you think of another profession, which requires often one person to manage up to thirty different and shifting agendas in a small and often ill-designed room?

With the benefit of your experience to date and as you think back to the initial training you received, did it adequately prepare you for managing the range and nature of difficult behaviours you have encountered? When have you received specialist guidance to cope with having your judgement questioned by a young person in what is, at best, a very public setting and at worst sometimes a hostile audience?

This book will provide you with reassurance and confidence that there are solutions to what may seem frustrating and emotionally fraught situations. Reassurance that it takes time, effort and strength of belief to become a truly effective classroom leader. Effective classroom leaders acquire, develop and refine their skills during the process of gaining experience.

Seeing how your confidence will grow, how you will sound more relaxed and feel more in control comes from being presented with a wide range of alternative practical strategies that really work in a format that allows you to integrate them comfortably into your existing practice.

Take responsibility

What, in the context of your classroom are you responsible for? Is responsibility the same as control? If there are things happening that you do not like in your classrooms and you do not take responsibility for managing them, you won't be able to change them. It is always easier to find reasons why we can't do something. Beware of giving mental space to problem-centred thinking that attributes causation and blame on parenting skills, the home environment, scarce resources, school management, the National Curriculum, Government Policy, OFSTED, etc. While we can't control how Nathan spends his time in the evenings, or the fact that he comes from a violent and dysfunctional family and arrives in school tired and very hungry, we can take responsibility for how we respond to this baggage and how we manage his behaviour. Pay attention to what you *can* do something about. That's what we mean by taking responsibility. If what you try doesn't work – do it differently. That's also what we mean by responsibility.

Take action

To bring about change you have to actually do something that is different. To move along your journey to the kind of classroom you want, to becoming the kind of teacher you wish to be, requires that you do something to make it happen. Often this will mean taking a risk, leaving your comfort zone and on many occasions getting it wrong. Students do not expect teachers to be perfect. They expect them to be human, to be fallible and to be able to deal with it honestly and with humility.

There are a number of skills that are common to highly effective teachers. In this book you will certainly gain an insight into those skills but more than that you will have access to the beliefs that effective teachers hold about themselves and their students. Not just what effective teachers do but also *how* they manage to do it.

Keep an open mind

If, as you use this book, you spend time noticing what we haven't included, you'll be right. You will also be wasting precious energy. If you think about the times when some of the skills wouldn't work, you'll be right again.

If, however, as you read this book we engage you in thinking about things you'd like to be able to do, we recommend you devote energy and time into learning how to do them.

Chapter 1

BECOMING A LEADER IN YOUR CLASSROOM

True leadership must be for the benefit of the followers, not the enrichment of the leaders.

Robert Townsend, *Up the Organisation*, 1970

What is leadership?

What does the word conjure up for you?

> **Stop.**
>
> **Note down or draw the first thoughts and pictures that come into your mind when you think of the word 'leadership'.**

Don't read on.

Really do it!

Write down your thoughts NOW!

Leadership is the fabled elixir. It can turn failing schools into centres of excellence. It is the potion that enables head teachers to inspire competent teachers into becoming masters of their profession. It is the process by which you allow your students to become winners.

This book is all about helping you to become a competent classroom leader. We will look at the skills that are involved and how they can become relevant to every aspect of your professional life.

You recognise leadership as soon as you see it. We doubt that any of you found yourself with a blank piece of paper when we asked you to note down what the word conjured up for you (*You did do the exercise didn't you!*).

There is more to leadership than the public, glamorous images that many people conjure up.

Classroom leadership is present:

- in every classroom when students achieve things they didn't think were possible;

- every time a student grows, even just a little bit, in personal stature in your classroom;

- when a teacher simply holds up their hand and an entire hall full of students falls silent;

- every time your students look towards you for guidance or an example.

Why bother to become a leader in your classroom?

The answer is simple: to be able to achieve what is really important to you. By becoming an effective classroom leader you will enable the students you teach to grow both academically and socially.

Leadership is not a mysterious quality that is given to you during a secret ceremony. Leadership is simply a term which we use to describe the influential relationships that you have with others and the skills you bring to your interactions.

Classroom leadership is...

- the skills you have to manage yourself and to communicate with others;

- your ability to see the 'big picture' as well as the day-to-day detail and your skill in making sense of the relationships between the two;

- your ability to communicate your vision for your students in a way that attracts them to want to follow you.

Beginning the journey

Every leader is different. Leadership is not a specific set of fixed attributes that you have to squeeze yourself into. Becoming a classroom leader is about becoming more of yourself and, in doing so, inspiring your students to become more of themselves.

The notion of becoming a classroom leader may bring forth images of a charismatic teacher, leaping around the classroom, inspiring students through their infectious vitality – rather like Robin Williams in 'The Dead Poets Society'. That is certainly one, extremely energetic method of giving leadership to your students! Nevertheless, as Joseph O'Connor says so eloquently in *Leading with NLP*, 'The guide on the side is as effective as the sage on the stage'!

Leading is about influence. Leadership is about self-development. It is noticing the skills you have and learning new ones. Effective leaders then continue to refine these skills in the light of feedback. To become an effective classroom leader, the first person you will have to lead is yourself. Your students will not follow you if they don't believe that you know where you are going and that the journey matters to you.

What skills will you need?

You will need skills to:

- develop your own understandings and visions (for both yourself and your students);

- communicate these visions to your students;

- be able to see how your students work, what drives their behaviour and aspirations, and how you and your students come together as a classroom system;

- bring out the best in your students;

- create an environment within which students want to work, instead of feeling they have to work.

You will probably have realised that you are already demonstrating elements of these through your practice.

Our purpose is to help you learn from the best classroom leaders that we have met. We will show you how the best classroom leaders model the world they create for their students. We will give you access to a wide range of strategies from which you can select those that you feel will help you achieve your own, unique style of leadership.

The basics of leadership

Within the classroom, authority alone is not enough. Students will make very little progress both academically or socially simply by being told what to do. Authoritarian systems actively seek to discourage empowerment. Students with authoritarian teachers become disempowered learners.

How do you get your students to want to work if simply using authority will not be successful?

There are two extremes of approach that we have seen within classrooms. At one extreme is the 'natural growth' approach. This offers very little guidance or direction. It allows students to grow and learn through a natural osmosis.

At the other extreme is teaching by exception. These teachers only intervene if something is wrong – 'catch them being bad'! They provide no leadership or example to their students but simply believe that students will come to find the 'correct' way if they are sufficiently reprimanded for their mistakes.

These two styles are concerned with task and not direction. Classroom leaders empower their students. They show them *how* to learn as well as what to learn. The real test of your leadership is whether or not your students would still follow you if your authority disappeared.

Motivational matters

The simplistic view of motivation divides between two camps: adherents to the 'power of the stick' and 'followers of the carrot'.

The supporters of the stick believe that true motivation comes from avoidance behaviour – we are motivated away from the stick. The problem in class with this approach is that they frequently develop pupils who are good at avoiding the stick but learn very little.

'Followers of the carrot' believe that motivation comes through rewards. We are motivated towards the carrot rather than away from the stick. Is it effective? Yes, very frequently it seems to be highly effective. The problem comes when you run out of carrots! No carrot, no learning! Carrots represent extrinsic motivation and will only be successful while you are able to keep up a ready supply of tasty carrots. Everyone likes outward recognition of success – smiles, merits, certificates, etc. – and withholding these can be a great de-motivator but they are not the solution to the motivation problem.

Classroom leaders know a better way. They know that true motivation comes from inside their students – intrinsic motivation. Classroom leaders give their students what is important to them and not what is important to the teacher. Classroom leaders enable their students to gain pleasure from knowing they have achieved and grown.

And finally...

Classroom leaders lead by example. They 'walk the talk'. If you are setting out on the journey to become a classroom leader then the first person you need to lead is yourself. You must take charge of your own learning. Create your own vision and then set out to make it meaningful to your students. Learn from other classroom leaders and adapt their skills to help you inspire and motivate your students.

Classroom leadership is a skill you can learn.

To help you lay a good foundation for your journey, we suggest that you take some time to complete the exercises in Activities 1.1 to 1.3.

Key points

- Leadership comes from what you are within. It is not a bolt-on extra.

- Leadership is something given to you by others. You cannot give it to yourself.

- Effective classroom leadership enables students to grow both academically and socially.

- The specific skills involved include:

    - the ability to develop your understandings and visions

    - the skills of powerful communication

    - the understanding of what drives your students' behaviour and aspirations

    - the insights to help you understand your classroom as a system

    - the ability to seek out and understand feedback.

- Authority and leadership are not synonyms.

- Authoritarian teachers develop disempowered learners.

- Classroom leaders develop empowered learners by giving direction, meaning and purpose to learning.

- Classroom leaders recognise the power of extrinsic motivation but are constantly seeking out strategies to develop intrinsically motivated students. They do this by giving their students what is important to them and not what is important to the teacher.

Activity 1.1 – Creating your vision

Think back to the first time that you walked into a classroom to teach a class of pupils. If your experience was anything like ours, one of your immediate goals was to get to the end of the lesson still standing upright! That's OK. Teaching, particularly when you are new to it, is stressful, at times confusing, unpredictable, often daunting and always hard work! We are inviting you to look beyond your immediate survival needs. Go deeper. What was it that caused you to stand in front of a group of students who may, or may not, have been the least bit interested in what you had to say? What was it that you hoped to achieve for them? What was it that you hoped to achieve for yourself?

The old saying that 'When you're up to your neck in alligators, it is difficult to remember that you went in to drain the swamp' is probably never more true than in teaching! Yet, if you are to become an influential leader in your classroom, you need to keep a tight hold on your vision for your students' futures. If you want to constantly feel excited by the process of teaching, if you want to go home at the end of each day with a genuine feeling of satisfaction, then you need to be very clear about your vision. You need to get a tight hold on it, crystallise it, make very sure that it doesn't get eaten by the alligators!

The next exercise will probably take you some time. Allow several days, maybe longer, for it to mature. You can choose to keep coming back to it as you read through the rest of this book.

Don't just draw on your immediate experiences. You might like to also consider some of the following factors:

- teachers who influenced you in your past. What are the key characteristics that you remember? Bring a significant moment in your relationship with them to mind. What was special about it?

- which other colleagues that you work with do you admire for their leadership qualities? It may be your head teacher or another colleague that you know well. What is it about them that you would like to have as part of your own leadership style?

- what interactions have you had with students during which you felt that you were genuinely providing them with leadership? What was it that told you this?

- what other people have influenced you? What was it that separated them out from all the other thousands of people that you have encountered in your life? Why did you want to follow them?

- what examples of influential leadership have you read about or seen in the media. What was it about their story that motivated you? What was it that made you want to be just a little bit like them?

Activity 1.1 – continued

Gather information from as many other sources as you can. Make jottings and notes. Correct them and modify them. Look for those moments of 'magic' in your classroom that will tell you what is really important to you. Write down your thoughts and try them on for size in your classroom. It doesn't matter if they don't feel right yet, you can always grow into them.

When you are ready, use the questions below to begin to write your own, personal vision for yourself and your students.

- Imagine that you are now approaching the end of your career and that you have become a genuine leader within your classrooms. What evidence will there be to tell you this?

- What is it about your relationships with your pupils that tells you that you are ending your career as an influential leader? What else? What else?

- What will your students have been noticing about you that told them that you are someone worth following? What else? What else?

- Which of these qualities do you think your students will be especially pleased about?

- Who else will have noticed that your skills in classroom leadership have blossomed and what will each of these people have been seeing?

- What will have been the first small signs of change that will have suggested to you that your skills were improving?

Activity 1.2 – Create your own future

Now that you have begun to establish a view of yourself as a leader, let's begin to see what it will look like in reality. Take some time and really enjoy the experience of creating what your ideal classroom would be like. Build your ideas with full sensory experience. What would it look like? See the way it's set out, how you've used the furniture to help learning, the colours of the displays, any plants, posters, affirmations.

- What does it look like from your student's perspective?
- What's the first empowering thing they see when they walk in?
- What are people saying to each other?
- What type of language are they using?
- What opportunities are there to express ideas and share opinions?
- How are you explaining things?
- How is the language reflecting expectation, achievement and hope?
- In what ways will you and your students be handling conflict or confusion?
- What does it feel like to be in your classroom?
- Is this the same for everyone?
- In what ways is your classroom safe, both physically and emotionally?
- What do you do to make students look forward to returning?
- How would they feel when challenged by tasks or by taking a risk? What is the experience associated with making a mistake in your classroom?

Use the space below to draw, note down or choose any other way you prefer to represent your thoughts and responses.

Activity 1.3 – Plan your journey

I can't remember who said: 'if you don't know where you are going, you'll always get there,' but they were right!

In order to engage our brains in the most effective way we have to have some target or goal in mind. This book is about providing some key information to sustain your journey and it is just that – *your* journey.

While you are thinking about the vision you have created, of how you want it to be, imagine a scale of zero to ten.

- If your future vision represents ten on the scale, where are you now?
- What will you be doing more of or differently for your score to move up just one point over the next few weeks?
- What would be the first signs, however small, that things were moving upwards?
- What else would be different?
- Who would notice?

Apply as much detail as you possibly can to this process. Keep asking 'what else?'

Write what you will be doing differently in the space below.

Questions for professional development

What do you feel about the topics covered in this chapter?

What are some of the implications of the topics within your classroom?

What is most important for you to remember from this chapter?

Chapter 2

THE EMOTIONAL CLIMATE

Emotions enrich; any model which leaves them out is impoverished.
Daniel Goleman, *Emotional Intelligence*, 1996

In this chapter we will explore the many ways in which our emotions and those of our students contribute to the climate of the classroom.

- Have you ever found yourself in a situation that didn't generate some degree of emotional response?

- What are the emotions which being in your classroom generate and how powerful are they?

- Are they the same for you and your students?

- Are they positive and empowering emotions or negative and resentful ones?

> **Think of a time recently in class where things didn't work out quite as well as you'd expected. Maybe there was some conflict or argument or maybe the work didn't engage the students as you'd hoped it would. As you think back to that time, notice what's happening in your body. It's likely that some or all of the feelings that were present at the time have returned.**
>
> **Have you ever woken up and realised that today is the day you have your favourite class and felt a sense of positive anticipation, looking forward to a lesson that has the exciting buzz of learning? What happens when you think of the next time you will take this class?**

As you thought of things that have already happened or haven't happened yet, you naturally accessed some feelings that you experienced at the time even though you were somewhere else doing something different. This is a perfectly normal phenomenon.

Could this also be true for your students?

In considering the emotional climate of a classroom we are exploring the connections between learning, behaviour and the brain. It is obvious to suggest that the behaviour of the people in the classroom will have an effect on the emotional climate and yet we cannot consider behaviour in isolation. Behaviour is not random or accidental, it is a response to a physical sensation, a thought process, a belief or a range of stimuli from whatever activity we are engaged in at the time. As classrooms, by definition, are learning environments, the process of learning and the emotional response we have to that process will enhance or hinder the classroom climate.

- **How would you describe the emotional climate of your classroom?**

- **What do you consider to be the most effective conditions for learning?**

- **How do your ideas about the two questions compare?**

As effective classroom leaders, we have to consider the emotional climate of our classrooms as carefully as we consider the intellectual and physical environments. In fact, research into the brain and how it learns suggests that learning cannot take place under conditions of stress or coercion.

If we make the reasonable assumption that people work best and learn most effectively in a positive emotional environment, how would this be true for your classroom? The following question is one we ask ourselves on a regular basis and we suggest you do the same now.

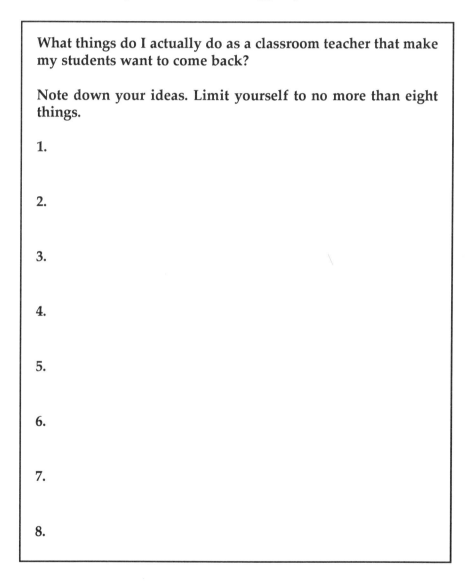

What things do I actually do as a classroom teacher that make my students want to come back?

Note down your ideas. Limit yourself to no more than eight things.

1.

2.

3.

4.

5.

6.

7.

8.

The emphasis in this question is on us as classroom leaders and managers. In what ways can we make a contribution towards creating the emotional climate necessary for effective learning? A head teacher colleague describes it as the difference between:

'Oh good it's geography!' and *'Oh God it's geography!'*

Factors affecting the classroom climate

Balancing encouragement with correction

How would your students describe you on your normal days? How would they assess the balance you achieve? Our experience suggests that the balance is skewed towards correction. Clearly, this is a generalisation and you only need to be concerned if this applies directly to you but when you ask your class to settle down and they begin to do that, who are the students you tend to talk to first? The ones who are slowest, the ones who haven't stopped talking or taken their coats off? Do you comment initially on those without a piece of equipment before noticing just how many are organised?

Could it be true that on occasions we take for granted the majority of students who simply turn up on time, well equipped, get on with the tasks and make our job considerably easier? *'Anyway, that's what they are expected to do. Why should that demand some recognition or even appreciation?'*

You may remember being given some advice early in your career such as 'Don't smile until Christmas' and 'You have to show them who's boss'. We hope you have realised what useless advice this really is. When you started your new job what would it have been like if no one had smiled at you for three months? If no one demonstrates some recognition and acknowledgement for things you do both at home and work – getting your reports in on time, cooking a meal, etc., how do you feel about that?

In our classrooms, we play a game called 'catch them being good'. It's very simple. You periodically stop what you are doing, scan around the room and comment on students making good choices and useful contributions. How have you reacted to a student who informs you that they 'like Maths now', or says 'You're better than our last teacher!' 'That was good, can we do that again?' Its important to remember that children are neurologically wired up in the same way as adults – we all like to be appreciated.

Building rapport with students

To build effective relationships requires effort, commitment and skill. It requires that you enter someone else's world in order to influence support and lead them. By establishing rapport, you are making an essential connection with someone at an emotional level. You are willing to share part of you and they are prepared to invest themselves into the dynamic.

There are many ways in which effective teachers build rapport with their students. Learning and using their names and greeting them in the corridor or lunch hall are simple examples. Showing genuine interest in not only things they do but also in them as fellow human beings. It is about consciously looking for and appreciating the skills and resources they possess.

Building rapport can be done subtly through matching or mirroring the behaviour of others. Respectfully, matching their smile, their tone of voice and its pace can help connect you to a person. Mirroring some of their actions, nodding of heads, facial expressions, raised eyebrows, hand gestures and so on are all ways of establishing rapport.

When you are in rapport with someone, the process of leadership, the nature of influence that you possess is significantly enhanced. Quite simply, you feel comfortable and develop a sense of trust with that person.

It is important to recognise that speaking respectfully, being pleasant and friendly and responsive to students' ideas is not in anyway incompatible with setting boundaries through an agenda for learning and behaving in the class. Nor is it at odds with using negative consequences which are fair and related when students make inappropriate choices that infringe the rights of others.

Connecting students to hope

In his book *Emotional Intelligence*, Daniel Goleman cites experiments that indicated how important hope was to performing tasks and learning effectively. Indeed, some people consider that hope is one of the most powerful motivating forces there is. As teachers, it is vital to our students' success and the emotional climate of the classroom that a sense of optimism prevails. You could describe it as having high expectations of yourself and others, as a way of taking responsibility or even our resilience when mistakes occur. At the heart of a hopeful learner is a belief system that says *'I can do something about this situation and I want to.'*

Students who appear to act without hope tend to interpret mistakes as simply being part of their own pathology – *'that's just the way I am'*. It is an appropriate analogy too for your journey to becoming a confident classroom leader. If you believe that making mistakes is a healthy part of gaining experience as a teacher and that by responding to experience and modifying what you do in the light of the feedback will move you closer to your vision, then that's exactly what will happen.

> *If you think you can or you think you can't, you're right.*
>
> Henry Ford

In Chapter 4 there are some detailed ideas of how you can use language powerfully to connect people to hope and before you turn to it...

- **Consider some times in your life where you helped somebody to be more hopeful or optimistic.**

- **Have you noticed when you have done this in class?**

- **What was that student's reaction to you? Did it add something to your relationship?**

- **If it helps, write down what you actually did to help this person.**

Keeping working relationships intact

Bill Rogers (1994) describes this process as 'repairing and rebuilding'. As in all relationships things do not always run smoothly and according to plan. When you consider the variety of needs and personalities with which you skilfully interact on a daily basis, it's inevitable that some conflict occurs.

Getting the relationship back on track is not difficult and really only involves normal teacher behaviour. It's a series of simple skills such as asking a student who you've moved for not working (and now is) 'How's it going? Do you need some help?' If you receive a grunt or a glare in response, you will recognise that there is still some stress there and you would want to give it a bit more time. Moving off with a casual, 'OK Dave, let me know if you do', doesn't buy into any kind of struggle the student may seek and keeps the door open for when he is ready.

In this simple and effective way you are building the classroom climate in two powerful ways. Firstly, you are demonstrating clearly to the student that you don't hold grudges. In other words, you accept the mistake or disruption as something different to the person. You don't accept the behaviour, which interferes with the rights of other students to learn, and this student is still welcome in your classroom. Secondly, you are modelling in a powerful and obvious way, how effectively to deal with resolving conflict. These are important lessons for children of all ages and we believe it is a fundamental professional responsibility of teachers to help students acquire these key skills.

Working with the notion of choice

On those occasions where you have caught yourself saying, 'Well, I had no choice', what kinds of feelings generally accompany the statement? Perhaps an impression of powerlessness, maybe a feeling of being coerced or manipulated, a sense of not being in control? They don't seem to be compatible with a positive and empowering emotional climate. Contrast the above with situations where your sense of self-determination was high. Maybe you were given a task, discussed and agreed outcomes and then were left to work through it the best way you knew how. You knew that help was available if you wanted it but it was your choice how you met the outcomes.

In Chapter 3 we will explore in more detail the impact of choice in the dynamics of classroom management. For now we would simply ask you to consider how widely choice is evident in your current working practice.

- **Do you give the opportunity for your students to make choices about how they present their work to you?**

- **What different opportunities can they make use of to show you they know by becoming more aware of their own learning styles and preferences?**

- **In terms of behaviour, do you expect to have to control the students or do you make explicit that they are accountable for their behaviour?**

- **How frequently do you refer to the 'good choices' your students make.**

Considering safety and confidence

Any environment where you do not feel emotionally or physically safe will not be a place you look forward to being in. It will create physical sensations of anxiety such as headaches, sickness and bodily tension which leads to a feeling of emotional fragility.

What is it about your classroom that allows people to feel safe? We know that it is important to feel safe in class for effective learning to occur, but what is it important to feel safe about in class? A key idea here is how we establish a framework in which it is an expected norm that mutual rights will be respected. The principles and processes of how to set this up and make it work are detailed in Chapter 3.

By definition, learning is about doing something new and challenging in which there is a clear element of risk. How do you ensure students feel as comfortable as possible about taking a risk in your class? How comfortable do you feel about taking a risk in your class? What we are describing here is the ability to move out of our comfort zones, to attempt things in a different way, to acquire some new knowledge and in the process make some mistakes.

- **What is your definition of failure?**

- **How do your students perceive failure?**

- **In what ways can you lead your students to feeling more comfortable with getting it wrong?**

- **What conditions and attitudes have to be present for getting it wrong to be a positive experience?**

- **When was the last time you had evidence of a student feeling OK with getting it wrong or not being able to do something?**

- **What was it you did that made that easier for them?**

- **What is the difference between failure and a mistake?**

Helping students feel part of the class

Rudolph Dreikurs (1998) cites the work of Alfred Adler, a Viennese psychiatrist as suggesting that a core desire of human being is to belong in a social and intellectual sense. All of the ideas described in the book will make a contribution towards a student feeling part of the class and comfortable in engaging in the activities of the class. However, this is not always the case from the start. The practical strategies in Chapter 6 will support you in managing student behaviour in a way which helps them feel part of the group at the same time as maintaining a learning agenda..

Focusing on what people are doing well

When you go home in the evening what balance of your time is spent considering all the things you did today that worked, the many areas, tasks and interactions in which you succeeded? Surely you don't over-focus on those few things that were difficult!

If you look for things that are not working you will always find plenty of them. Instead, make an active choice to notice the things that people do that help construct a positive emotional classroom. Notice what you are doing when things are going well. Pay attention to how you move, the way you speak, the feelings that are going on inside. How are you able to do these things? You will know from Chapter 1 that the ability to notice the skills and qualities you have and how you use them is a key feature of being an effective leader.

Equally, start looking for the resources your students show you. Think of your most difficult student and make a list of three things they do well that makes a useful contribution. At first, you might have been tempted to say they don't do anything. They're always interrupting or never sit still. Keep with the process because no one 'never' or 'always' does things. Sometimes we have to go back to really small chunks. Sometimes not being as difficult as at other times is an improvement and an indication of some skill and certainly an indication of the ability to make a choice.

Teacher style

The way in which we approach our teaching will have a significant impact on the climate of the classroom. When we describe a particular style we are aware of the fact that they are stereotypes and also that we will fit different styles on different days and in differing circumstances. Essentially we mean the style that we adopt most of the time, our characteristically recognisable style, and the one that our students would be most familiar with.

An autocratic or demanding style of teacher will have powerful beliefs about their role. They will often rely on power or status to influence classes. The words 'make', 'control' and 'must' feature heavily in their beliefs.

'Children must respect me because I'm a teacher.'

'If I let one get away with it, they'll all be doing it.'

Their behaviour will also manifest hostility in language patterns, the use of sarcasm and humiliation to coerce students to do as they are told, to obey.

As you can see, this doesn't fit with what we have described as an emotionally positive classroom. In fact, you can be guaranteed stress and anxiety because when these unrealistic beliefs conflict with reality, an autocratic teacher will work even harder building conflict and confrontation to *make* their dysfunctional beliefs true.

An ambivalent or uncertain style of teaching can be confusing. By definition it will be difficult to be a leader from a position of uncertainty and ambiguity. Often, though compassionate and wanting very much to influence, there is indecision about the precise role of a classroom leader and the nature of authority. This teacher's behaviour will be characterised by a non-assertive tonality, a lack of congruence and a tendency, as Kounin (1977) puts it, to 'overdwell' on disruptive behaviour.

A confident classroom leader will recognise that students make choices about their behaviour. They will not invest their personality in discipline infractions by interpreting them as a personal attack. Rather, they will use a framework such as the 4Rs approach outlined in Chapter 3 to respond to student behaviours. Their focus will be on celebrating success and their manner will communicate a passionate belief that their students will be successful.

You will do this by constant positive feedback and by working to a plan based on your vision for your classes. Above all else, you will have a clear understanding that the only thing that you can control in class is your own behaviour. You will seek to guide, encourage influence and lead by the rapport that you work hard to create and sustain with your students. You will recognise that teaching is a skill-based activity and that the most effective teachers are those who are the most effective learners.

Key points

- People learn better when they feel relaxed and happy.

- Everything you do can affect how your students feel.

- Catching people being good is very powerful.

- Positive relationships hold the key to leadership.

- Everybody has a choice – teach students to make useful ones.

- Making mistakes is important.

- Responding to feedback is vital.

Questions for professional development

What do you feel about the topics covered in this chapter?

What are some of the implications of the topics within your classroom?

What is it most important to you to remember from this chapter?

Chapter 3

ESTABLISHING YOUR CLASSROOM AGENDA

'That's not a regular rule: you invented it just now.'
'It's the oldest rule in the book,' said the King.
'Then it ought to be Number One,' said Alice.

Alice's Adventures in Wonderland, Lewis Caroll

What is so important about agendas?

The agendas that you set within your classroom wholly determine your success in implementing your classroom leadership plan. They will set the daily climate for the academic and social growth of your students. They will be a key deciding factor in setting the extent to which your students can develop their sense of empowerment. Therefore, to a great extent, this whole book is about agenda setting.

This chapter looks at an essential and key aspect of setting your personal classroom agenda – your 4Rs framework of Rights, Responsibilities, Rules and Routines. We will show you how you can develop this framework, via supportive and corrective interventions,

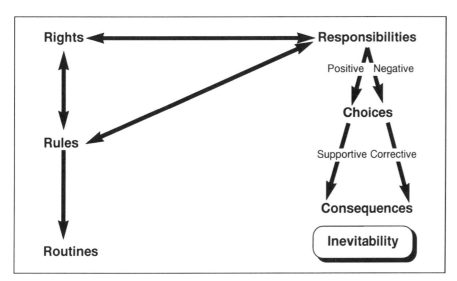

Figure 3.1   The 4Rs Framework

to enable you to establish the learning climate that all of your students will see as being in their best interests.

The first R – Rights

What is your justification for labelling certain behaviours as 'unacceptable'? Simply relying upon your authority – 'Because I say so' – is not good enough.

When you provide leadership in your classroom, you need a clear, conveyable, framework within which you can make decisions about your response to student behaviour. A framework which students can both understand and buy into.

Your decisions need to be firmly based upon your judgement about the extent to which a student's behaviour supports or infringes one of four basic rights. These are:

1. your students' right to learn
2. your right to teach
3. everybody's right to safety (physical and psychological)
4. everybody's right to dignity and respect.

Basing your behaviour management on these four basic rights enables you to go beyond the 'Because I said so!' approach. It enables you to deal easily with the student who instinctively responds to your corrective interventions with *'Why not?'* or *'Why shouldn't I...?'*

While all four rights are a key feature of your teaching, your overriding area of professional responsibility lies in the protection of everybody's right to safety. Above all else, when your students enter your classroom they must be sure that they will be safe both physically and psychologically. No learning will take place with students who do not feel safe.

The second R – Responsibilities

Rights and responsibilities are inseparable. Your focus must be upon enabling your students to make positive choices about their behaviour. The notion of encouraging pupils to choose responsible behaviour is so crucial to effective classroom leadership that we have not only devoted a separate section to the language of choice below, but it will be a recurring theme throughout the strategies in this book.

The third R – Rules

If you have conveyed to your students that you will be focusing upon the due rights of all and that you will be setting out to achieve this by encouraging your students to take responsibility for their own behaviour, then your rules will establish the framework within which this is possible.

You must make a distinction between rules and routines. Routines refer to the administrative aspects and procedures necessary to help any complex organisation resist the slide into chaos. Routines are dealt with under the next section – the fourth R.

These are the three basic rules we have found to be most effective in our classrooms:

1. Follow your teacher's directions.
2. Keep your hands, feet and objects to yourself.
3. No swearing, name-calling, put-downs, etc.

The first rule is about the protection of the right to teach and the right to learn, while the next two are about the protection of physical and psychological safety. The third rule also protects the right to dignity and respect.

Whichever way you choose to display your rules to your students, make sure they are a prominent feature in your classroom. Don't have them tucked away among other display items. Make them big and bold. Let your students be in no doubt as to their central importance.

If you are not entirely comfortable with simply having these three rules in your classroom then feel free to come up with your own. However, bear in mind the following points:

- They must refer directly to your rights and responsibilities focus.

- They must be few in number. No more than three rules for Key Stage 1 and then add 1 more rule for each additional Key Stage up to a maximum of six rules in Key Stage 4. If you have too many rules you, and your students, will forget to follow them.

- They must be phrased in a way that ensures your students are clear what you mean. 'Treat everybody nicely' is nowhere near as explicit as 'No swearing, name-calling, put-downs, etc.'

- They must deal with behaviours that you can observe within your classroom. Don't have a rule about homework, for example. Save this for one of your routines. You must be able to 'catch' your students following your rules.

- They need to be understood by your students and actively taught to them.

For now, one final word on rules. You may well have noticed that we have not suggested that you negotiate your rules with your students. Always take time to explain the rationale behind your rules to your students but the rules themselves are best kept as non-negotiable. If we are to provide effective leadership for our students then we need to take the clear responsibility for establishing the framework within which that leadership can grow and develop.

The fourth R – Routines

Routines are essential to the smooth running of your classroom. Be very clear about the routines you need in order to help your students become successful.

For example, you will need routines for entering and leaving the classroom, how you get work out and put it away, moving around the classroom, asking and answering questions, and so the list goes on!

Your routines will represent the specific set of behaviours that are at the core of helping your students become successful. The more precise you can be about your routines the more likely it is that your students will follow them. Saying to your students:

'I want to see everybody sitting properly' leaves itself open to a wide variety of interpretations.

However: *'I need to see everybody with their pen and pencil on the desk, hands on the desk, mouths closed and eyes on me'* is far more likely to bring about the desired response.

> **Think through a typical week's teaching. Begin with first thing on Monday morning and work your way through to last thing on Friday. Note down all the regular, day-to-day activities that you need specific routines for, as well as taking account of those activities which may only occur infrequently.**
>
> **Now, take each routine and think through the specific behaviours you would see your students displaying if they were being successful in the activity. For each of these, try to determine a limited set of directions that will concisely convey to your students those behaviours that you wish to see. Choose observable behaviours and avoid the use of negatives such as 'Don't talk' or 'No walking about'.**
>
> **Begin a list of your essential routines and their directions. Keep it close at hand for the next week and add to it as more routines occur. Become aware of how much you need to teach your students so that they can become successful.**

As well as the day-to-day routines, you will also need to be alert to the routines that you may only use infrequently such as going to the library, having a visitor into the room, going to assembly. Particular attention needs to be given to teaching these routines as your students will have plenty of opportunity to get out of their good habits in the times between their use.

Remember that it is not sufficient to simply tell your students what your specific routines are. You need to both actively teach them to your students (with younger students this may involve getting your students to role play the routines) and to constantly state them as expectations before moving into an activity

Avoiding conflict with choices

The language of choice is your key to empowerment. Within your 4Rs Framework, it directly underpins responsibilities.

The language you use in your classroom is so crucial to your students' success that the whole of the next chapter is devoted to this topic alone. In this particular section we just want to alert you to the power of that simple word 'choice'.

Much of the language used in classrooms is the language of disempowerment – phrases such as: *'Jamie, if you don't settle down to work then I will send you to sit over there.'* or more simply: *'Helen, put the book down and go back to your seat.'*

In a whole variety of small, subtle ways teachers are conveying the message that they can make pupils do things. If Jamie or Helen should decline your polite request for alternative behaviour you will be one step further towards engaging in a power struggle in your classroom!

You can rapidly begin both to teach genuine responsibility and simultaneously reduce conflict in your classroom by simply starting to use the language of choice. Here are some examples that may serve to make our point clear.

- 'Jamie, if you don't settle to work then I will send you to sit over there' becomes: 'Jamie, if you choose not to settle to your work then you'll be choosing to sit over there.'

- 'Helen, put the book down and go back to your seat' becomes 'Helen, I need you to choose to put your book down and go back to your seat.'

- 'Michael, thanks for working hard to day' becomes 'Michael, thanks for choosing to work hard today.'

- 'Kyle, if you don't do your homework then you'll be in detention tomorrow' becomes 'Kyle, if you choose not to do your homework then you'll be choosing to be in detention tomorrow.'

And so it can go on. We haven't found a classroom interaction yet that couldn't be translated into the language of choice – should you choose to do so of course! We will deal in more detail about the specific skills of implementing choices in Chapter 6.

Consequences – the big C

Simply reminding David that he has a choice about his behaviour will not guarantee that he will choose appropriate behaviour. This is where your consequences – supportive and corrective – fit in. The consistent application of consequences is essential to your students' learning process. We call it the 'night follows day' principle of teaching appropriate choices. If a student makes an appropriate choice about their behaviour then you ensure a positive, or supportive, consequence. If a student makes an inappropriate choice about their behaviour then you ensure a negative, or corrective, consequence.

Corrective consequences do not need to be severe. It is not the severity of your consequences that determines reductions in inappropriate behaviour, it is that they will inevitably happen. Inevitability is far more important than severity. How do you think many adults would alter their driving behaviour if they knew that *every* time they exceeded the speed limit they would be pulled over and spoken to by the police!

Keeping them close to the event

Keep your consequences as closely linked to the actual behaviour as possible. This is especially true with younger students and those who have difficulty making appropriate choices. We recognise that giving immediate feedback, supportive or corrective, is not always a practical option and it is sometimes necessary to introduce some form of delay. Keep delays as short as possible even with students in Key Stage 4.

Making consequences logical and fair

Using the language of choice when you apply a consequence (particularly a corrective consequence) establishes a logical connection between the student's choice of behaviour and the applied consequence. You increase the likelihood of your corrective action having the desired effect.

The consequences you apply to student choice need to be seen to be fair and proportionate to the student's action. In particular, you need to be seen to be fair between and among students. You must have no favourites.

Making rewards rewarding

We talked about the difference between extrinsic and intrinsic rewards in Chapter 1. We emphasised the need to understand the essential role of intrinsic reward while recognising the necessity for extrinsic rewards. For students who are learning about responsibility, the use of extrinsic rewards is essential.

You can provide positive, supportive feedback to your students in one of four ways:

1. Social reinforcement

This is simultaneously the most powerful and the most easily used form of supportive feedback. It can be a smile, wink, nod or thumbs up. Frequently it will be verbal. 'John, I like the way you're choosing to work today. Well done'; 'Thanks for...'; 'Suzy, that's really great. I like...'; etc. Verbal feedback is best given as a mix of specific – the actual behaviour – and global – your pleasure at it being displayed. The power of these forms of supportive feedback is dealt with in detail in Chapters 2 and 4.

2. Symbolic reinforcement

This includes everything from drawing smiley faces on a student's work, through stars, stickers and stamps, to more formal displays of success such as charts on the wall. If the star, sticker or stamp is seen by the student as a genuine symbol that you care about them the effect (even with older students) can be dramatic. One word of warning about wall displays of stickers: be careful that they do not become a display of 'Let's spot the student who doesn't get any stickers!'

3. Special activities

These will be choices offered to your students in recognition of their achievement. Examples of these might be playing with a special toy, sitting with a friend to work, missing a homework or gaining free time.

4. Token economies

These can be introduced as a system whereby individuals or groups can accumulate tokens (points, stars, etc.) towards a bigger, more tangible reward. This might be whole-class free time, a pizza party (appealing to the stomach is a very basic form of positive feedback!), or even something as simple as a few raisins. Token economies can be especially successful in enabling you to settle whole classes into a routine of good choice.

Integrating your supportive feedback

Providing systematic, supportive feedback takes practice. You need to get used to integrating your feedback into the rest of your teaching routines. While you are leading the 'up-front' phase of your lesson you can be supporting hands-up behaviours. While you are moving around facilitating cooperative groups you can be noticing and supporting appropriate social behaviours. Get good at integrating high-frequency social feedback into every aspect of your teaching. Your own, personal, supportive feedback will come from your increased enjoyment of teaching.

> **Turn to Activity 3.1 at the end of this chapter and make a list of 20 opportunities that you might find, during a typical teaching day, to give your students positive, social feedback. (We've started you off with five but you might like to discuss with colleagues to help you reach your target figure.)**

Corrective interventions

Despite your best efforts to work within a clear rights and responsibilities focus and the attention you give to positive recognition, there will still be times when your students make inappropriate choices about their behaviour. When this occurs you must know how to deal with it quickly, fairly and firmly.

You will use a wide range of corrective interventions to work with pupils who make an inappropriate choice about their behaviour. Many of these will be dealt with in detail in Chapter 6. They consist of a wide range of low-level corrective or re-directive behaviours which are supported, when necessary, by a range of more formal, structured consequences.

In this section we will concentrate upon the formal structure of corrective interventions that you will need together with some of the principles behind their implementation.

Effective formal consequences:

- are things that the student would rather avoid happening;
- don't violate their best interests by harming them physically or psychologically;
- contain some form of inconvenience factor such as sitting away from the group or delaying the student at the end of a session;
- are structured and progressive.

The most effective way of organising your more formal, corrective interventions is in the form of a hierarchy. Each stage of your hierarchy represents an increasing level of inconvenience or structure for the student. The notion of a discipline hierarchy is central to the DfEE's guidance on the effective use of sanctions in schools and is a highly successful approach used in many of the schools we work with.

Two examples of a hierarchy might be:

For Key Stages 1 and 2:
- **Stage 1 – a warning**
- **Stage 2 – five minutes aside from the rest of the group (time-out)**
- **Stage 3 – two minutes behind at the end of the session**
- **Stage 4 – parents involved**
- **Stage 5 – exit to another class for remainder of the session and parents involved**
- **Severe behaviours – exit to another class for remainder of the session and parents involved**

For Key Stages 3 and 4:
- **Stage 1 – a warning**
- **Stage 2 – five minutes aside from the rest of the group (time-out)**
- **Stage 3 – two minutes behind at the end of the lesson**
- **Stage 4 – Head of Department involved**
- **Stage 5 – sent to another class to work and letter home**
- **Stage 6 – exit to member of the Senior Management Team (SMT) and parents involved**
- **Severe behaviours – exit to a member of the Senior Management Team and parents involved.**

You will notice that each of these hierarchies begins with the use of a formal warning:

'John, you have chosen a warning. If you continue to choose to…then you will be choosing to spend five minutes aside from the group. I'd like you to choose to (state desired behaviour).'

This gives the student a further opportunity to change their behaviour.

Each of the hierarchies contains a provision for dealing with students who are seriously and/or persistently infringing the rights of others and whose behaviour it would not be appropriate to deal with by systematically working your way through your hierarchy – normally this would be because of infringements of the right to physical or psychological safety. These more severe behaviours would result in moving directly to some form of exit.

These hierarchies are only examples. You may be working within a school that already has an agreed hierarchy. If you are then use it. If you haven't already got an agreed system then you will need to develop a hierarchy that both fits with what is practical within your particular circumstances and within your school's other existing frameworks. If you are developing your own hierarchy then make sure that you clear any potential involvement of other colleagues before you need their support.

Be prepared to do what you say

An essential point to make with regard to the application of corrective interventions is that once applied they must *always* be carried through. You must not back down (unless of course you have made a mistake when a gracious apology may be appropriate) or let students off the consequences of their choice. You must be the certainty in your students' lives. They must know that you mean what you say.

Exits from the classroom

As in all matters, you will obviously have to work within your school's existing guidelines for exiting or removing students from the classroom. Nevertheless, there are some key points that need to be born in mind:

- Exiting a student is not a way of abdicating your responsibility towards your students. Exiting a student is simply a way of allowing others to regain their ability to enjoy their rights. The clear message the exited student needs to receive is that the exit is not your way of getting rid of them, you are simply putting them on 'hold' until you can have a supportive, structured conversation with them (see Chapter 6).

- Having to exit a student is not a sign of 'weakness'. It is part of the reality of teaching. It is simply an indication that sometimes, despite our best efforts, some students are hurting so much inside that they find it almost impossible to function within a busy classroom.

- Whenever practical, parents (or carers) need to be informed that their child had to be exited from the classroom. We would go as far as to say that the only reason a parent should not be informed is if there are known reasons why such an action would place the student at risk (child protection issues, etc.).

- Keep records. This is essential when considering students within all Key Stages, but is especially true in the secondary sector where a student may be experiencing severe difficulties across a range of lessons. If any student is regularly moving through to exit on discipline hierarchies then there is clear evidence that the strategies being employed are not effective and something different needs to be done. (Many of these alternative strategies are the focus for our book *Creative Pastoral Care*.)

Getting the balance right

In Chapter 2 we talked about the essential balance that you need to keep between supportive and corrective behaviours. It is all too easy, when we feel under pressure, to select more and more negative interactions with students. If you choose to fall into this trap you will set an increasingly negative agenda in your classroom. Your students will associate your room with somewhere they go to fail. They will become increasingly disempowered.

Effective classroom leaders plan to 'catch them being good'. They consciously make an effort to use more positive than negative interactions with their students. In particular, they ensure that they consistently give positive feedback for appropriate choices concerning social behaviour as well as academic behaviour. They create a classroom atmosphere where students learn that they go to win. They create empowered students.

> **Activity 3.2 contains a format for planning out your rules, rewards and corrective intervention framework. Using the information from this chapter to guide you, draw up the plan that you will use to set your key classroom agenda.**

And finally...

Don't think that your 4Rs framework and the associated consequences – particularly your formal sanctions hierarchy – will do your behaviour management for you. It won't. It is simply a system.

The only thing that will make a difference in your classroom is your skill as a leader. Effective behaviour management, as with everything else in teaching, is about micro-skills. All your 4Rs framework will do is to provide you with a clear structure within which you can constantly improve your micro-skills.

Key points

- The 4Rs framework gives you your key focus for agenda-setting.

- A focus on the due rights of all helps students make sense of your behaviour.

- Rules should be:
  - few in number
  - supportive of rights
  - fair and unambiguous
  - taught and used.

- A key focus for your behaviour is to help students learn responsibility.

- We learn responsibility through being empowered to make choices.

- Routines should:
  - be clear
  - represent the essential behaviours necessary for your students to become successful.

- Positive consequences should:
  - be inevitable
  - be used frequently for positive choices
  - represent emotional feedback
  - be given for social as well as academic behaviour.

- Corrective consequences should:
  - be inevitable
  - be mild
  - be applied as close to the behaviour as possible
  - be fair and logically connected
  - not violate the best interests of the student
  - be progressive.

Activity 3.1

Twenty opportunities to make my students feel good by praising:

1. Entering the room quietly

2. Tidying their desk

3. Making a good effort with work

4. Helping a fellow pupil with their work

5. Bringing the right equipment

6. _____

7. _____

8. _____

9. _____

10. _____

11. _____

12. _____

13. _____

14. _____

15. _____

16. _____

17. _____

18. _____

19. _____

20. _____

Activity 3.2

My essential behaviour management framework

Essential, rules to protect rights – maximum 3 for Key Stage 1 to maximum 6 for Key Stage 4

1. _____

2. _____

3. _____

4. _____

5. _____

6. _____

Examples of supportive feedback that I might use (in addition to any whole-school procedures):

Social feedback:

_____

Symbolic feedback:

_____

Special activities:

_____

Whole-class or group feedback:

_____

My hierarchy of formal corrective actions (maximum 6 including warning and exit):

   1. Warning

   2. _____

   3. _____

   4. _____

   5. _____

   6. Exit to _____

For more severe behaviours:

   Exit to _____

Questions for professional development

What do you feel about the topics covered in this chapter?

What are some of the implications of the topics within your classroom?

What is it most important to you to remember from this chapter?

Chapter 4

THE POWER OF LANGUAGE

It is impossible not to communicate.

Richard Bandler

Developing congruence

You are constantly communicating with your students even before any words are spoken. From the moment the students first entered your class, they were receiving messages from you. Those messages would tell them a considerable amount about you. True, they were only first impressions and making first impressions leads us to fit people into our experience, make a judgement and then run habits and patterns of response.

The information that allowed your students to make judgements about you came from:

- what you were wearing

- where you stood and how you stood and moved

- facial expression and coloration

- tonality and inflection when you spoke

- any gestures you made

and many other subtleties.

Teaching is about communication. It is about getting yourself and your students into the correct state mentally and physically to learn and then managing that state. Your effective communication will help students make better choices about their behaviour, become motivated and sustain that engagement.

To be an effective communicator requires that you develop a sense of congruence. Personal congruence is your ability to have your verbal and non-verbal language fully supported by your beliefs and values. To achieve congruence you will need to be committed to what you are saying and doing. If you tell a student that you are confident he or she will do well are you convinced? How important is the tone of your voice?

Say out loud *'Michael sit down'*, in as many ways as you can.

Remember to use upward and downward inflection. What difference does this make?

Remember to change your state. Make your body tense and say it. Pull a funny face and say it. Lean casually against a wall and say it. Think of a time you were annoyed, happy, relaxed and say it. Does how you feel affect your communication? Does your communication affect how you feel?

Notice what happens when you change your body position. Is your communication different when standing rather than sitting?

In your classes, when you say *'Michael, sit down'*, do you expect him to comply? How does Michael understand that?

Things we do with language

If how you are communicating is not bringing the results you want – do something different. Effective classroom leaders have the flexibility to alter what they are doing in the light of the feedback they observe. They will have built for themselves a wide choice of strategies and plans for managing both the learning and the behaviour of their students. They will have rehearsed parts of their strategy, especially the tonality and inflection of the language patterns. Above all, as they move through their repertoire they will be entirely congruent. In other words, they will have a clear understanding of the outcome they wish for and a confident belief that they will achieve it.

These key ideas will make a rapid difference to the effectiveness of your communication with your students.

Be responsible for your communication

A common response, when other people don't react in the way we expect or can't seem to understand what we want, is to blame *them*.

We have already mentioned the flexibility that effective communicators demonstrate. On most occasions, when we tune in to the (usually obvious) feedback that the class or individual students haven't quite grasped what is required of them, we will explain things again or in a different way. We will recognise the receiver's needs.

- What about the occasions when this is not true?

- What's different about those times?

- What are your feelings when this happens?

It is likely that these are situations where it appears more difficult to elicit the response you want. If you choose, then these situations can be very frustrating and we complete the cycle because frustration is a major roadblock to communication. Recognising that you are responsible for your communication is summed up well by a principle of Neuro Linguistic Programming (NLP) that says, '*The meaning of your communication is the response you get.*'

Develop your sensory awareness

Very often when we are communicating, especially in a naturally stressful, multi-dimensional and unpredictable environment or, as it is more commonly known, a classroom, we tend to be more aware of how we are feeling. Effective communicators notice what's happening around them. They notice changes in the physiology of students such as muscle tension, frowning, facial colour and breathing patterns. They are aware of tonality and inflection in voices and, as we will look at later, the actual words chosen. Doing this provides you with essential feedback to guide your own choices in communication. It allows you to match what's happening with your appropriate and considered response.

Sensory awareness allows you to:

- use a non-verbal and calming gesture to students arriving a little too hyped up;

- recognise a student arriving who's upset and acknowledge their feelings – often this is enough;

- notice those students who are getting prepared for the class and acknowledge them for doing so;

- tune in to variations in class, e.g. noise levels rising and falling or spotting when an activity is losing the groups interest;

- effectively play 'catch them being good' (see Chapter 2).

Get into state first

We use language in all its forms to create images and states in other people. As teachers we aim to enthuse, captivate and engage our students with the excitement and relevance of what's on offer. If we don't get into the correct state first we are not going to lead our students there.

Imagine you are in class right now...

- **Two students are arguing heatedly. It is intruding on the class work. You need to do something.**

- **What is your preferred outcome?**

- **What state would be most effective for you to go into?**

- **How will you do that?**

- **What will your intervention look and sound like?**

- **How do you want the two students to experience it?**

- **As you are not actually in the classroom, how easy is it to go into that state right now?**

Write down no more than three examples of a time when you've consciously altered your state to influence an outcome.

N.B. Consider other areas of your life too but don't have too much fun!

If in doubt – check it out

Part of the process of taking responsibility for your communication is having enough information to alter your communication accordingly. We can become more skilled, through practice, at picking up sensory clues to aid our communication. Using questions to elicit additional information is also a valuable strategy.

- Which part of this is easiest/hardest for you?

- What would help you understand this even more?

- What's stopping you finishing this work?

- What would you like to happen that would help you calm down?

Without access to this information, it becomes easy to make assumptions that we really know what everyone else is thinking. This is a potential roadblock in effective communication because everyone makes sense of the world in his or her own unique way. If we presuppose that anyone has the same 'mental map' of the world as us it leads us into judgements and behaviours that are not always helpful or effective in arriving at our outcomes. We can't remember where we heard this but we liked it:

When you 'assume' you make an 'ass' out of 'u' and 'me'.

A recent story about a Year 2 boy from one of our workshops illustrated this concept beautifully for us.

B: Can I go to the toilet?

T: What's the magic word?

B: Abracadabra!

The important thing here is that they are both right! They are just running different perceptual models of the world.

Make directions clear and positive

Pay attention to your thoughts and the feelings in your body as you read the following two paragraphs.

In all of the chapters we have been making suggestions of things for you to try out in class. We have made the suggestions because they work and will have a positive impact on your skill as a confident classroom leader.

In a few places in the book you might find where we have alluded to the pitfalls of teaching and warned you not to do these things. If you don't do these things it will prevent you getting some problems in your class.

Note down some of the different responses and experiences.

What questions, opportunities and possibilities did each generate for you?

One of the most powerful ways that language can influence positively is to use language which is positive! Experience and research tells us that situations in class that escalate are usually preceded by a series of demands. Often it is the lack of clarity in those demands or instructions that contributes most to the escalation.

When you are giving directions to students either to explain an activity or because you need to correct or refocus their behaviour it is essential that you describe what you want them to do rather than what you want them to stop doing: 'stop talking and pay attention' is more effectively expressed as 'facing this way and listening quietly'.

Reframing your language from 'don't' to 'do' is important because it:

- accurately describes a satisfactory outcome

- has clarity and is unequivocal

- provides an alternative course of action.

Have you ever asked a student to stop doing something and find that they've followed your instructions but are now doing something else equally irritating?

The key to using positive language lies with the idea that in order to understand language, we have to trigger an internal response. The word *'don't'* only exists as a linguistic tool. It has no internal experience associated with it. Try and experience a *'don't'*. If we add some more information such as, *'don't shout loudly'*, what exactly is your experience now?

Please don't think of something red right now!

Write some alternatives in the margin to these phrases:

Stop calling out	**Stop running in the corridor**
Don't forget your homework	**Don't be late**
Don't speak to me like that	**Don't worry about the exams**
Stop tapping your pen	**Don't spit**

Internal dialogue

Everybody talks to themselves and contrary to the old adage, it is not the first sign of madness. In fact, it is a very sophisticated way of checking if what is going on in the world makes sense to you or more accurately how you make your sense of what's going on in your world.

In understanding the power of self-talk, you will be extending the skills and opportunities for leading your students to a state where they can more effectively lead themselves. This is a key concept in our view of leadership. In many ways the test of leadership excellence is how effectively our students take charge of themselves when we are not there.

Some students will have been running an internal dialogue for some time about their particular experiences of being in a certain subject. If the experience is not a rewarding one then the self-talk may well be a response to some physical sensation such as a headache or feeling sick or just a sense of discomfort. It doesn't take a great leap for this negative self-talk to become a belief. Vocalised, the thoughts might be:

> *'Because this is an unpleasant experience in which the experience I understand as success eludes me I must be no good at it.'*

The role of a classroom leader is to present examples, in a genuine and sincere way (i.e. congruently), that run counter to the negative self-talk. To provide experiences and opportunities followed by feedback which in some small but persistent and consistent way challenge the negative beliefs. It's as if the evidence gives a student permission to believe something new and hopefully empowering.

The language of hope

Here are some reminders:

- Hope is a powerful motivational force and an essential component for success.

- Language triggers an internal response.

- Internal motivation is often more powerful than external motivation.

- Language is often processed non-consciously.

- We can beneficially influence people's emotional state with congruent use of language.

- A person's state directly affects their capability to learn.

- A person's state drives their behaviour.

Here are some practical applications and ways of using language to connect people to their source of hope.

Encouragement and praise

The idea of praising people to make them feel good is not new. There is a fuller discussion about the nature of praise in Chapter 3 in connection with rewards and consequences. We think praise is excellent. We like being praised and provided it is genuine and sincere, i.e. carries an emotional lift with it, there is no limit on how much we can take! However, what about those occasions when students don't accept your praise? We have experienced some students, having received some praise, actually screw up their paper and start again. That's not part of the plan. Why would they do that? Maybe it's because they felt patronised or embarrassed. Maybe it ran counter to *their* opinion of the quality of the work.

You've now come across one of the difficulties of praise. It works most effectively when you and the student share your 'mental maps' of the world. Because it is an external motivation, i.e. we decide what's worthy of praise and when to give it, it may not generate the more powerful internal motivation, the sort that just leaves you with a sense of this experience being anywhere from OK to WOW!

Encouragement is a slightly different way of giving the feedback students need. It is a more precise use of language and aims to create more of an internal response. The difference is probably best illustrated by the following examples.

This is praise:

   S: **I've finished my graph Miss, is it OK?**

   T: **Excellent! Good work! Go on to No 2.**

This is encouragement:

   S: **I've finished my graph Miss, is it OK?**

   T: **Let's see. You've got a title, labelled the axis and plotted the points in a straight line. You really understand graphs. I bet you're proud of that. Have a go at No 2.**

In what ways were the two transactions different? What similarities are there?

What feelings would each generate for you if you are the student?

As you describe to the student what you can see in their book you are simultaneously flagging the qualities of a good graph. There is no sense of judgement here. You are then inviting the student to feel good (if they don't already!) about what they have done.

- Does this sound a good idea to you?

- How would this have to be delivered to be congruent?

- Can you see yourself using this idea?

- How easy would it be for you to feel congruent?

- How would you manage that?

Reframing

There's a line in Hamlet that says,

'There's nothing either good or bad, but thinking makes it so.'

The idea of reframing is that experience in itself only becomes meaningful, can only generate a response in us, when we interpret it. The way we interpret it will have an enormous impact on whether we feel good or bad. Incidentally, feeling good or bad, depressed or happy is a choice we make, based on how we frame any given experience.

We are assuming that you will want to try out these strategies in your class at some point (obviously not all at once!)

- **What will happen when you use a strategy and it doesn't work?**

- **What do you do now with the strategies you already use?**

- **Will that situation be a failure or will it be a learning experience?**

- **Will it inhibit you from doing it again or will you use the experience as feedback to tune and enhance the skill?**

You have at least two responses to the same situation. One will limit your development as a classroom leader and one will enhance it. Which one depends on the frame you place it in.

Here are some more examples of reframing:

- Getting 50 per cent correct rather than half wrong.

- Having 28 students in your class that you are working effectively with rather than the two that you're not (yet) (or maybe some of the time).

- The student you acknowledge for making good choices after playtime rather than the antisocial ones before play.

- Making a list of everything you've achieved today and then being able to feel great about ticking off all your list before you go home rather than making a list of all the things you haven't got around to.

- A student we worked with recently told us that he was *'the fourth worst student in the year group'*. This he told us with a sigh and hunched shoulders. We moved him on to achievement thinking by excitedly saying *'Wow! How did you manage that?'* His evidence was that he had been sent out of class four times this term and the winner had been sent out nine times. Through casual questions about the number of lessons in the week and how many weeks he'd been back at school we were able to say, *'so this means you managed not to get sent out of 96 lessons'*. His reaction? A wry smile and slow nodding as the reframing sunk in. This was followed by more animated language as he reeled off a list of other things he'd managed to do well at this term – like being at school every day and being on time every day and many others. He left the room with a handshake (his decision) and a true teenage swagger.

Language that wounds

Differing perceptual models

We have seen how language can trigger a reaction in us. We have all had some experience whereby language has evoked a very powerful emotional response.

'I really love you Dad!'

'Your car's been stolen.'

Yet it is not the words that do this. After all they are only words. It is our interpretation of the words that generates the emotion.

Supposing we told you that you were the worst teacher we'd ever met? Would what we said hurt you? No, because words can't do that. What has the potential to hurt you is how you choose to make sense of what we said and how you carried on talking to yourself *inside* your head. In other words, your internal dialogue.

Much of what is said in class is incidental language. It's incidental and accidental because we rarely consider its significance. We don't have to make a conscious effort to engage in everyday talk. We know the meaning and inference of what we say. We know what we mean by what we say. But does the other person?

You enter the staff room and flop down, sigh deeply and say, '*I am soooooo depressed*.' Your colleague is likely to say, '*Yeah, I know what you mean!*' Actually they have no idea whether to make you a cup of tea or call the Samaritans because you are both operating from your own perception of a word called 'depressed'.

The intention of this section is to allow you to be aware of how what you may say off the cuff and without meaning anything unpleasant can be interpreted differently. It is to allow you to be aware of presuppositions in your language.

If you said to a student, '*Why don't you add a bit more to your story?*' there is a presupposition that they haven't written enough.

Here are some of types of things teachers say. What presuppositions or underlying assumptions might they carry?

'*What have you done wrong now?*'

'*Look, you're just being stupid again aren't you?*'

'*How many more times do I have to tell you?*'

'*For goodness sake grow up and act your age!*'

'*That's typical of you isn't it? Just giving up like that.*'

In what different ways might the student interpret these comments?

Secondary behaviours

Secondary behaviours are nothing to do with secondary schools although of course they occur there. In fact, they occur anywhere that you find people. Secondary behaviours are what we use to avoid taking responsibility for something we've done – usually a mistake of some sort. They are how we deflect the 'heat' of actually acknowledging that we are less than perfect. Secondary behaviours are not the preserve of children either and we're sure that as you read this you will remember situations in which you behaved in a similar way.

In many ways, secondary behaviours are linked to presuppositions and experience. With students, they will have a learned response that under certain conditions that they will recognise from an adult's tone of voice, their body language and the circumstances of this transaction, they are going to feel uncomfortable. What circumstances are we talking about?

Getting 'told off'. We guess most of your experiences of being 'told off' have not been enjoyable. Maybe you didn't get your reports written in time and the Deputy Head spoke to you about it. Our guess is that you tried to justify it in some way. Can you hear yourself saying.

'But the photocopier jammed', maybe in your head you were also thinking, *'Yeah, well what a ridiculous timescale you set. You want to try teaching the timetable I've got!'*

Or perhaps you were late meeting your partner and deflected your bad timing with, *'You should have seen the idiot crawling along in front of me.'*

For students in class the experience is usually more uncomfortable than the ones we described above because:

- it is in public

- it is in front of their friends

- they know from experience that they're going to feel bad about it.

Their non-conscious response tends to be to justify or deflect the inevitable by a process called 'getting your retaliation in first'. This will take many forms that we know you will recognise instantly.

Some of the responses will be non-verbal in the way the student will sigh, tut, pout or toss their head about.

Many, of course, will be verbal. Imagine this scenario. You are working hard to manage the class. It seems a bit harder than normal and you feel frustration creeping up.

'Jenny. Facing this way and mouth closed, thanks.'

This is said reasonably pleasantly and the reply comes back:

(Deep sigh) 'I was only talking about this stuff you're making us do'.

All of a sudden the creeping has turned to a charge. Our internal dialogue starts work overtime. *'How dare she. What a totally unreasonable reaction. She's lying, I heard her chatting about a party!'*

The frustration becomes tension somewhere deep in our stomach. This feeling interacts with our mouth. Our mouth interacts with Jenny. Hey Presto! Welcome to the field of behaviour management called,

'GUTS TO GOB'

Why do we react this way? 'Guts to gob' reactions are caused by a mix of emotions but, we believe, the most significant among them is the feeling that, for a split second, control of the lesson has slipped away from us and passed to Jenny. This causes our stress levels to rise. This is uncomfortable so to counteract this we seek the quickest way we can think of in our emotionally charged state to regain control – we interact with Jenny.

'I don't care what you were talking about! PAY ATTENTION!!!!!'

You will find some valuable ideas for responding to secondary behaviours and avoiding 'guts to gob' reactions in Chapter 6.

Key points

- Be congruent in your communication.

- Develop your sensory awareness to the communication around you.

- Work to make language positive, giving clues as to what you want them to do.

- Language builds hope, without which there is nothing.

- Use language to create possibilities rather than problems.

- Stay focused on primary behaviours.

- Language has a direct impact on self-esteem.

- Keep careful track of how you talk to yourself.

Questions for professional development

What do you feel about the topics covered in this chapter?

What are some of the implications of the topics within your classroom?

What is it most important to you to remember from this chapter?

Chapter 5

ESSENTIAL PROTOCOLS

In the province of the mind, what one believes to be true either is true or becomes true.

John C. Lilly

Your essential protocols are the guiding principles that you hold to be true and which enable you to create your classroom discipline (supportive and corrective) in the way you want to. They stem directly from your vision for your students (see Chapter 1).

In this chapter we are going to share with you the key protocols that we hold to be true. Some of them will sit comfortably within your current ways of working, others might take more conscious effort for you to adopt. All of them have been addressed in depth elsewhere in this book but we have gathered them together here as a form of precursor to the next chapter which examines the range of practical interventions that flow from them.

1. Work within, and actively teach, your 4Rs framework

It is not sufficient to have the 4Rs plan inside your head. It needs to become an integral part of your classroom practice. Refer to rules and rights in both supportive and corrective transactions.

Actively teach your students about the framework and then go through it at regular intervals. Regularly teach and reinforce your routines and the specific directions that stem from them. Don't assume that your students will remember them.

2. Plan for good behaviour

Effective classroom leaders do not leave their behaviour management to chance, good luck or a belief that 'something will occur'. They have a behaviour management plan.

Your plan will take account of the wide range of supportive behaviours that you will use to encourage and correct. In common with all good plans it will be 'safe fail'. It will recognse that the best laid plans sometimes go awry. You will already have allowed for this possibility and you will have a plan to cope with it!

Good plans need rehearsal. You will need to practise your plan by 'walking' through it mentally. You might even like to rehearse some of your scripts.

3. Model the behaviours you wish to see

Always remember that your students look to you for an example of legitimate adult behaviour. Teachers who use verbal or physical hostility in their classrooms are legitimising the very same behaviour in their students. If you want your students to treat you respectfully, the process must start from you. If you demonstrate respect for your students then they will reciprocate.

4. Discipline with dignity, correct with compassion

Create win–win situations. Allow your students a graceful way out. Don't back students into psychological corners. When involved in a corrective discipline transaction with a student it is important that you speak in a way that protects your students' feelings of self-worth. Sarcasm, put-downs, verbal attacks on the person are sometimes all-too-familiar strategies adopted by some teachers. They are an unfortunate consequence of a lack of effective skills.

5. Empowerment comes from believing you are responsible for your own behaviour – you have a choice

We have said much in this book about the language of choice and about strategies for developing empowerment within your students. Remember that helping your students towards genuine empowerment is probably the single greatest gift you can give them.

6. Keep your focus upon primary behaviours

Choose to ignore the whining, pouting, sulky behaviours. Look beyond the disrespectful body language. Use partial agreements to cut through the minor verbal challenges such as *'We were only talking about the work'* or *'She was talking as well'*.

7. Actively build trust

Do not assume that your students will automatically trust that what you are doing is in their best interests. Their previous experiences of adults, both in and out of education, may lead them to very different conclusions. Be consistent. Be predictable. Make sure that you always demonstrate that you have the best interests of your students at heart. Show an interest in them as people both in and out of your classroom. Accept that both you and they have 'off days'. Trust is something that develops over time.

8. Grudges break relationships – repair relationships as often as necessary

Just because a student has made some poor choices about their behaviour doesn't mean that you have to avoid saying anything positive to them. Some teachers seem to think that because they have had to correct a student's behaviour it means they have to avoid all forms of praise from that point on! In fact, the very opposite is true. As soon as you have chosen to have a corrective transaction with as student you should be looking for opportunities to 'catch them being good'. It is your professional responsibility to repair working relationships with your students as quickly as possible.

9. Follow up or follow through

Always follow through with the choices your students have made. This is particularly true when students have chosen a sanction. Striking bargains or backing off in response to whining appeals undermines your credibility as a leader.

10. Actively take steps to reduce confrontation

Realise that the only person you can control is you. You can manage the behaviour of your students but you can't control it.

Recognise that when a student challenges your directions they are not making you less of a teacher. They are simply doing what young people have always done (and will probably always do): challenging adults. Stay calm, use your rehearsed language patterns – particularly the language of choice, stay focused upon your 4Rs framework and utilise your range of planned interventions.

11. Keep in touch with your identity

Some teachers fall into the trap of psychologically investing too much in their discipline transactions. It is as if they have coupled their entire manhood or womanhood to their ability to get a student to do what they have told them! This is not healthy. Life is too short! Having a bad lesson or even a bad week doesn't change or negate the great and unique qualities you possess. Don't personalise your corrective interventions.

12. Hold high expectations

Remember that one of the single greatest determinants of students' eventual educational achievement will be the expectations their teachers had of them. If you have low academic and social expectations of your students you will convey this unconsciously through your intonation and body language.

Your students will live up, or down, to your expectations. Choose to expect your students to be successful.

13. Actively develop and use a wide range of intervention strategies

The more choices you feel you have in responding to examples of unacceptable behaviour, the more relaxed you will become and the more confident you will feel.

14. Ensure your corrective consequences are fair and logical

Wherever possible, make a direct connection between the consequences the student is choosing and their actual behaviour. Be seen to be fair. Don't issue whole-class consequences because of the behaviour of a few. Don't enforce rules with one student that you waive for another.

Make sure that your consequences are likely to influence future choices – both positive and negative. Make sure that you apply your corrective consequences with inevitability rather than severity.

Questions for professional development

What do you feel about the topics covered in this chapter?

What are some of the implications of the topics within your classroom?

What is it most important to you to remember from this chapter?

Chapter 6

PUTTING IT INTO PRACTICE

He who dares wins.
Del Trotter, *Only Fools and Horses*

Introduction

This chapter will extend your repertoire of choices. It contains a selection of some of the strategies that we teach on our workshops. We have included a sufficient range that we believe will help all teachers manage the vast majority of what happens in class. Again, if you look for what isn't here, you'll find it! We also recommend that teachers talk to each other openly about what they do. It is a vital balance to share what worked and to celebrate that fact as well as discussing concerns.

These strategies are field tested and they work. They work in all phases of education and in all types of school. They also work in other countries and if you work hard they work at home too!

Core skills

There are common threads, which all successful discipline transactions with students contain. Whatever the specific strategy you use, work to build these skills into it until you become unconsciously skilled at them.

Pause

It takes time to stop doing something and think about, understand and then do something else. You are more likely to achieve compliance if you deliberately allow time for this process. Putting a pause after you call the student's name and before you give the direction helps to gain and then sustain the attention. It's also OK to have to repeat a student's name a couple of times. It's worth remembering that the style, inflection and tonality you use to call someone's name will have a direct bearing on their mood when they give you eye contact.

Positive directions

This is dealt with in more detail in Chapter 4. Here we would just remind you that directing students to what you want them to choose to do, rather than what you want them to stop is more effective.

Allow take-up time

The image we like is of a spotlight lighting up a student each time you call their name and speak to them. If we are refocusing a student's behaviour, the longer the spotlight stays on, the greater the potential for feeling discomfort. Further or extended eye contact can also be construed as a challenge. Turning away and breaking eye contact when you are up-front in class or moving away as you are working the room is a subtle yet very powerful way of conveying that:

- the transaction is over and there's no more to be said

- you are confident that the student will follow the direction

- you *expect* them to comply

- you care about their self-esteem and will turn the spotlight off quickly

- you do not dwell or add 'heat' to your directions.

Use non-confrontational techniques

Here are three key reasons to avoid confrontational behaviour management:

1. It doesn't work.
2. If we use it, it not only models it but legitimises our students using it.
3. It damages self-esteem and many of your students will be vulnerable already in this area.

Confrontation can be perceived from many angles:

Tone of voice

It is hard not to let growing frustration affect your tonality, especially if you have repeated an instruction several times for the same 'offence' (see our 'Rule of three' strategy later in this chapter). You know that 'guts to gob' reactions are counter-productive and leave you feeling uptight, and that a calm, assertive tone conveys expectation, demonstrates you are in control and have chosen to manage student behaviour within a rights-enhancing framework. You may not know *how* to carry it off.

We favour the 5-5-5 method. When you feel and sound tense, breathe in for five seconds, hold it for five seconds and breathe out for five seconds. This is not only very relaxing it literally gives you fifteen seconds breathing space to frame your response.

Invading personal space

Again, stress can direct to us to less than helpful behaviours. Keep space between you and the student. Consciously slow down movements (5-5-5 is helpful here too).The behaviours below will contribute to your and the student's stress levels:

- leaning over a seated pupil

- standing too close (like boxers before a contest)

- moving quickly towards a student.

Confrontational gestures

- finger wagging, and in some cases, prodding

- banging desks

- hands on hips and leaning forward.

Make a conscious effort to work out how to be relaxed. Try pretending – it works really well. Try substituting an open hand for the wagging finger.

Expect and act as if students will comply with your requests

The expectation of compliance is vital to classroom management. Effective teachers work very hard to behave in a way which gives a congruent message that they are confident the student will see the reasonable nature of our request without feeling attacked personally and will cooperate with us.

Managing secondary behaviours

We have given you an outline of what secondary behaviours are in Chapter 4. You know also, that if you choose, they can be extremely frustrating. Here are examples of secondary behaviour you will be very familiar with:

T: Andrew, facing this way and listening, thanks.

S: But I was only talking about the work (sigh).

T: Don't give me that. I heard you talk about the party (gotcha!).

S: They were talking too. Tell them then! (you're picking on me).

Sometimes it goes on...and on...and on.

'This is boring!'

'I wasn't...'

'Other teachers...'

'Can't make me!'

'Don't care anyway!'

Working with the principle that agreeing with someone is a superb way of defusing conflict, and recognising that we need to focus on the primary behaviour, i.e. the talking, we have found this simple phrase to be tremendously useful.

'Maybe...and...'

T: Andrew, facing this way and listening. Thanks.

S: But I was only talking about the work (sigh).

T: Maybe you were and I want you to face this way and listen. Thanks.

If students persist with the secondary behaviours and you've repeated the direction, move to a consequential choice.

'Andrew, if you choose to argue with me, you're also choosing to stay back after class.' Now apply take-up time.

Progressive interventions

In most cases we have found it easier to explain the strategies through dialogue. You then have the choice of whether you just read the ideas, or visualise how you will use them or you can simply have a go either role playing them with a colleague or trying them with your classes.

Low-level strategies

Planning to ignore the behaviour

Plan:

- the kind of things you are able to ignore

- how long you can ignore them for

- what you will do if ignoring it doesn't work.

It is important to combine the ignoring of the behaviour with emphasising and praising the students who are behaving well.

'Thanks for putting your hand up, Brian. What's your idea?'

Reaffirming the rule that is being broken

'What's our rule for lining up, Neil?'

or with slightly more assertion when needed:

'We've got a rule for asking questions, Stephanie, and I expect you to use it'.

Using non-verbal signals

Using non-confrontational gestures relating to noise level, keep writing, calm down, sit up straight, arms folded and so on are gentler and less intrusive on occasions than a verbal instruction. We can also use smiles, thumbs up, nods, silent applause and so on to offer praise. With older students, the unobtrusive use of praise is often preferred. At lower primary and nursery level, holding the child's hand as you redirect the behaviour can, if used appropriately, be a powerful and calming non-verbal accompaniment.

Giving brief instructions

'Ian sit down now. Thanks.'

'Yeah, EastEnders *was good wasn't it? Back to work now Jenny. Thanks.'*

'When...then'

This can be useful as a way of linking behaviour to outcome and recognising not only the reality of situations but also emphasising accountability for one's behaviour.

'When you talk loudly then I can't teach.'

'When you're in your seat then I'll check your work.'

'When we've got our coats off then we'll have a story on the carpet.'

'When this part of the lesson is over then you can explain your side to me.'

Medium-level strategies

Re-focusing with questions

'How are you getting on?'

'You need to finish this by the end of the lesson. Are you on target?'

'Is there a reason you're out of your seat?'

'Do you need some help here?'

Maybe . . . and (see page 70)

This is a very powerful strategy for those situations where you sense the student could become argumentative.

The 'Rule of three'

If you repeat instructions more than three times without increasing seriousness you are actually teaching students that it's OK not to do as you ask.

'Faizur, facing this way and listening. Thanks.' would be step 1

'Faizur, the instruction is facing this way and listening. Thanks.' would be step 2 and delivered with a more assertive tonality, increased eye contact and maybe a non-verbal gesture. It also contains the word 'instruction'.

'Faizur, if you choose to keep talking you're also choosing to take a warning. I want to see you facing this way and listening now. Thanks.'

Using humour

There is no doubt that relaxed humour is a very powerful way to defuse conflict. Of course there is a fine line between humour and sarcasm. It's worth remembering that it's alright to laugh at ourselves too.

'Double what' questions

The purpose of the questions is to move the student to ownership of the required and acceptable behaviour.

'Rifat, you're out of your seat, what are you doing?'

'Nothing.'

'What should you be doing?'

'I dunno.'

'You should be finishing you graph. Back to work now. Thanks.'

Removing the audience

Taking the student to one side to speak quietly, or squatting or kneeling down to their chair level and giving a whispered reminder or instruction helps to take the sting out of situations and maintain the student's self esteem. Sometimes it may be necessary to take them just outside the room. If you do, make sure you are in the doorway and in view of the class rather than the student.

Giving simple and realistic choices

'Brian, if you choose to keep talking, you're choosing to have a warning.'

'Nadine, if you choose not to finish your work in class you're choosing to finish it in playtime.'

Following up on the student's choice

We have discussed the importance of the students being encouraged to take responsibility for their behaviour by recognising they are making a choice. A key feature of establishing this principle is how consistently we reinforce the choices the student actually makes. If their choice is the consequence outlined then it is imperative we follow through with that.

High-level strategies

High emotional arousal and confrontation often accompany high-level strategies. It is even more crucial that the principles and core skills apply here. Some techniques for refocusing arguments are:

- Calm yourself before you try it with others.

- State specifically what you want the student to do.

- Use the 'rule of three' and emphasise they will have a right of reply when calm.

- Remind them of the right to respectful treatment.

- Matter of factly state the consequence of continuing the conflict.

- Agree you can't make them – emphasise they are choosing.

- Give take-up time.

- Apply the consequence and expect compliance.

- Return to the start, increasing the immediacy and seriousness of the consequence.

Using in-class withdrawal

If possible move the student in class, ideally away from others. If this is not practical you may consider some form of 'time out'.

Giving a choice

Give the student a choice between compliance or a deferred consequence. This may be a formal detention, a parental contact or the involvement of parents and or another colleague such as a Key Stage Coordinator, Year Head or Deputy Head.

Following through with the given consequence

Time out

A brief exit from the room for three to five minutes to give the student a chance to calm down and reflect. It is important that this is done as part of a planned and taught intervention and is not connected with the idea of a 'sin bin' or 'naughty corner'.

Using agreed exit procedures

See Chapter 3 and 'What to do if it doesn't work'.

Following up after class

Often it is necessary to defer corrective conversations with students to a time outside your lesson. This strategy has many advantages:

- It allows both you and the student some 'cooling off' time. This is especially important if the student's behaviour has raised the emotional temperature.

- It means that the conversation can happen away from an audience – often a factor for consideration with older students.

- It gives time for you to consider your response.

- It gives some time in class for you to repair relationships with the student, thus making the likelihood of a successful conversation so much the greater.

The following structured conversation (with your own personalisation) can be extremely powerful with students of all ages as part of your after-class follow-up:

- Thank the student for staying back:

  'Thanks for staying behind Martin. I need a word about...'

- Be sensitive to their feelings:

  'I understand that you're probably still a little bit angry and also probably a bit worried about what I am going to say.'

- Focus upon the specific behaviour that you observed (with some students you might like to mirror their behaviour back to them – done in a way that protects their dignity):

  'What I saw you do was...'

- Relate the behaviour to your 4Rs framework:

  'That's against our rule for...and stops the rest of the class...'

- Invite feedback:

  'Can you explain why you...?'

- Restate the rule infringed and emphasise responsibility:

  'I can see that you...Nevertheless, we have a rule which says...and I need you to be responsible for following it.'

- Look towards a different future:

  'If that happens again, what could you choose to do differently?'

- Support the student if describing alternative:

  Either: 'That's a really good suggestion and I know you can do it.' or: 'How would it be if...?'

- Part with a positive expectation:

  'Thanks for talking with me. I know we're going to get along fine in the future.'

What to do if it doesn't work

As we have said before, the only guarantee in teaching is that it is hard work! Life has a habit of taking you by surprise. What can you do if, despite your best efforts, the student continues to be disruptive? Here are a few suggestions that you might like to consider:

- Stick to your discipline plan. Do not be concerned if you have to move a student through to exit and then follow them up afterwards (see Chapter 3 and 'follow-up' strategies earlier in this chapter).

- Seek the immediate support of your colleagues. This might mean that you have to send another student to fetch a colleague to come to your room and support you with a student who is choosing particularly difficult behaviour. Be confident about sending for help if you think a situation is getting out of hand.

Common workshop questions

The following are a sample of the most frequently asked questions on our workshops.

'I like the idea of working within the 4Rs framework, but I've been teaching my class(es) for just over a term. Can I introduce it now or do I have to wait until next September and start afresh with a new class?'

Obviously, the ideal situation is to introduce any system to your classes at the beginning of your relationship with them. That doesn't mean all is lost. Here are a two ways that we have used to introduce a new structure mid-year:

- Simply start using the language associated with the 4Rs framework without formally introducing the structure:

  'David, I like the choices you are making today. Thanks.'

  'Michelle, don't forget that everybody in class has a right to learn. I'd like you to choose to ... '

- Once your students become accustomed to the language, you can introduce the structure. Wait until a convenient point in your relationship with the class (the first lesson back after a break is a good time) and use part of a lesson as a 'review' of how you are working together. You can then easily introduce your new system.

'I can see how this applies to almost all of the students I work with but there are one or two that I just can't get along with. They make me so annoyed.'

Two things need to be born in mind and they both stem from the fact that we are working within the real world. Firstly, you can't like every student you work with. Just because you don't like them doesn't mean that you can't show them respect. The strategies in this book are based upon mutual respect not friendship.

Secondly, the reality of some student's behaviour is that they will make you annoyed, frustrated, even angry. The key lies in how you respond to these feelings. If you choose to allow your feelings of anger to manifest themselves in verbal aggression or slamming books down on desks then you will be legitimising the very same behaviour in your students. You need to model the behaviour that you would wish to see them use:

'Neil, your behaviour has made me feel very angry. I need you to sit there and I will come back to talk to you in a couple of minutes when I have calmed myself down.'

or even:

'Janet, I am feeling very angry about the choices you have just made. I need you to go to Mrs Williams' class for a short time while I calm down.'

'What about pupils who don't have the skills necessary?'

Redirection only works if the student you are redirecting is capable of displaying the behaviour. This situation is sometimes more of a concern if you are working with younger students but can also occur throughout the age range. If the student can't do the behaviour then it is our responsibility to teach it.

'What about students who are not competent English language users?'

It is not uncommon on our workshops for teachers to say something like:

'That all sounds great, but how do you use all of this language-based stuff with children who don't speak English?'

This again, is a difficulty more frequently encountered by teachers working with younger students There is not always an easy solution but here are one or two strategies that we utilise:

- Remember the power of body language. The language you use for your behaviour management transactions goes way beyond the words you use. Over-emphasise your gesture to accompany your re-directive words.

- Work out a core of essential phrases in your student's mother-tongue equivalent and then utilise the strategies we have listed and give yourself simultaneous translation.

'You've mainly talked about working with individuals. What do you do when the whole class is disruptive?'

Firstly, in our experience it is very rare for the whole class to be disruptive. It might feel like that but it is usually a significant, but vocal, minority who are causing difficulty. Obviously, intervening with effective strategies early on with individuals will help prevent things spreading.

If it is *genuinely* the whole class who are disruptive then the problem goes beyond both the scope of this book and the scope of almost all teachers to manage without a great deal of support.

Some strategies that you might try to help a small but significant group of students back 'on board' follow:

- If you are working in a secondary school, it is unlikely that you will be the only teacher having difficulty with this class. Ask around. See if you can establish a strategic plan that is common to all the teachers working with this group. Frequently, the person who is most likely to be able to coordinate a strategic plan is the Head of Year.

- Ask for support. One of the great frustrations that many teachers feel is that they can't get the whole class's attention in order to begin to re-establish a more orderly system. You might choose to enlist the support of a 'higher status' colleague such as a Head of Year or Deputy (anybody for whom the class is likely to become more orderly) to come into your room while you conduct a mini whole-class meeting. Don't ask them to conduct the meeting for you. One strategy that many teachers say works extremely well is to say something like:

  'Good morning Class 8. I've asked Mrs Williams to come into our lesson today because I need to have a conversation with you about the way we have been working together and I think it is important that she hears what we have to say.'

  You've now explained her presence while not implying to the class that the reason she is there is because you don't think you can manage them.

- Brutally ignore those students who are persistently calling out while, simultaneously being very specific in praising students who choose appropriate behaviours – 'Thanks for choosing to put up your hand, Jake.' Only keep this up for five or six minutes. While you are ignoring the shouting-out behaviours of Mark, Mary,

Wayne, Joseph *et al.*, you will be ready to 'pounce' at the first sign that they make a good choice so that you can reinforce it:

T: Yes Joseph. Thanks for putting up your hand, what have you got to say?

J: Nuffin. (big smile to his friends)

T: That's OK. Maybe next time. (smile and thumbs up)

He was just trying to find out if he could get your praise and now he knows he can, he will try it again (and so might his mates).

- In Chapter 3 we mentioned, as part of your supportive strategies, the idea of 'token economies'. This can be extremely powerful as a method of re-focusing groups or whole classes. It is simply a system of 'points mean prizes' building up to a class-wide reward.

Your role is to catch as many students choosing appropriate behaviour as possible and give points towards the eventual class-wide prize. As a 'rule of thumb', students in Key Stage 1 should achieve their prize within a day, Key stage 2 within two to three days. Key Stages 3 and 4 within a week to 10 days.

Also, if you do use this strategy, don't forget that the rewards must be genuinely class-wide. Even if Mark has not earned a single point he still takes part in the reward. Next time you use the system he will make his own points contribution.

- Work with the key 'power brokers'. Even if there appears to be a large number of students who are making inappropriate choices, there are usually one or two key students who lead while others follow. These are the students that, out of lessons, you need to focus your rebuilding strategies on. Sometimes talking to colleagues will help you establish the student's areas of interest or strengths so that you can begin to build a better working relationship.

The most important factor to bear in mind when working with difficult groups and classes is that *everybody* finds it difficult.

A word about change

Implementing change and performing new skills can be stressful for you and confusing for your students. We recommend that with the ideas and strategies you like best, you:

- have a go at them one at a time!

- practise and rehearse them at home or in the privacy of your own brain so that you can have an awareness of what they would feel, look and sound like when you successfully implement them;

- introduce them to your students on a day when you feel fairly buoyant;

- introduce them with your best class first;

- are prepared for your students to react differently from how you expected;

- avoid one trial learning, whereby if it doesn't work perfectly the first time, you ditch it.

Keeping a record

We also recommend, as an effective part of your personal and professional development, you keep a brief form of diary. This could be the odd note in your planner or something more formal – you choose.

One of the most powerful questions that we have found to be valuable is,

'If I tried this (particular skill) in my classroom what impact would it have?'

You then have to respond to all the various pieces of feedback you receive. If it works, do it some more and tell others about it. If it doesn't, think about why and then modify it.

REFERENCES AND RESOURCES

Entries that are starred (*) we would also highly recommend as invaluable resources to support your personal development.

*Dreikurs, R. *et al.* (1998) *Maintaining Sanity in the Classroom*. Bristol: Accelerated Development.

*Goleman, D. (1996) *Emotional Intelligence*. London: Bloomsbury.

Hook, P. and Vass, A. (2000) *Creative Pastoral Care for Difficult Behaviour*. London: David Fulton Publishers.

Kounin, J. (1977) *Discipline and Group Management in Classrooms*. New York: Holt, Rinehart & Winston.

O'Connor, J. (1998) *Leading with NLP*. Glasgow: HarperCollins.

*Rogers, B. (1994) *The Language of Discipline*. Plymouth: Northcote House Publishers.

Additional resources

These are not directly referenced in the text but we would highly recommend them.

Course

Brief Therapy Practice, 4d Shirley Mews, London, W9 3DY: E-mail: Brief3@aol.com They run regular courses throughout the country on 'solution focused' approaches.

Books

Applegarth, M. *et al.* (1997) *The Empowerment Pocketbook*. Hampshire: Management Pocketbooks.

Covey, S. (1994) *The Seven Habits of Highly Effective People*. London: Simon & Schuster.

Hook, P. and Vass, A. (2000) *Creative Pastoral Care for Difficult Behaviour*. London: David Fulton Publishers.

Howard, P. J. (1994) *The Owner's Manual for the Brain*. Texas: Bard Press.

HMSO (1989) *Discipline in Schools: Report of the Committee of Enquiry Chaired by Lord Elton*. London: HMSO.

Jensen, E. (1995) *Super Teaching*. San Diego: The Brain Store, Inc.

*O'Connor, J. *et al.* (1993) *Introducing NLP*. Glasgow: HarperCollins.

*Robbins, A. (1988) *Unlimited Power*. London: Simon & Schuster.

Notes

Notes